CONTENTS

5 TAXES

Printed in the United States of America

INVESTING

TURN YOUR LUNCH MONEY INTO $1 MILLION

Source: **Wayne Wagner,** chairman, Plexus Group, a Los Angeles-based consulting firm that advises money managers and brokerage firms. He is coauthor of *Millionaire: The Best Explanation of How an Index Fund Can Turn Your Lunch Money into a Fortune.* Renaissance.

In the booming stock market of the mid-1990s, when index funds outpaced virtually all other mutual funds, investors piled in. But, in a bear market, these passively managed funds lose their allure. Why track the market when it seems to be headed south?

There are many reasons why a single index fund is the only investment you'll ever need, says trading wiz Wayne Wagner.

Why should investors use index funds rather than actively managed mutual funds?

Because they work. In 14 of the 20 years from 1980 through 1999, index funds simply did better than the average equity fund. **TWO REASONS...**

• ***US stock markets are efficient.*** With so many investors and money managers following financial news, most stocks remain near their "fair" price. It's extremely difficult for a mutual fund manager to exploit price differences consistently. Index funds don't waste time trying to do better than the market. They just try to match it.

- ***Lower expenses.*** Index funds don't need expensive research staffs to make investment decisions—they trade to stay in lockstep with the index. Most index funds pass along those savings to investors.

Some S&P 500 index funds charge as little as 0.18% per year. The typical actively managed domestic equity mutual fund has an expense ratio of 1.4%. That difference adds up over time.

EXAMPLE: Assume that you invested $180 per month in two funds that each gained 10% a year over the next 40 years—before expenses. But one's annual expense ratio was 0.18%...the other's was 1.4%. The low-expense fund would earn more than $1.07 million...the high-expense fund, less than $749,000.

Any other advantages?

Yes, there are several...

- ***Simplicity.*** The biggest reason people don't invest isn't fear or lack of money. They simply don't know what to do. Strategies don't get any simpler than regular investments in an S&P 500 index fund.
- ***No worries about picking the right funds,*** stocks or fund managers.
- ***No hassles.*** With actively managed mutual funds, investors are warned to make sure a fund's performance isn't slipping and its focus isn't changing. And they're told to rebalance their portfolios at least once a year. There's no need to do either with a single fund.

Isn't it dangerous to put all your money into one fund?

With an actively managed fund, it would be dangerous. But S&P 500 index funds don't zig or zag. They serve as a proxy for the US stock market.

If you owned a portfolio of stocks, not mutual funds—and that portfolio contained shares of 500 of the country's largest firms—no one would say you were taking a risk. They would say you had an extremely diversified portfolio. The same is true for an index fund.

Why haven't all investors turned to index funds?

Brokers earn big commissions—and fund companies can charge much higher management fees—for actively managed funds, so their funds are marketed aggressively. Besides, index funds are not glamorous. At any given time, one sector leads the market, so certain managed funds will post eye-popping returns—short term. When your friends are swapping stock tips, no one is going to be impressed with your index fund.

Should investors also use bond index funds?

Bonds simply can't offer the high returns that long-term investors need.

For the 75 years through 2000, 30-year US Treasury bonds have had an average annual return of 5.3%. Large-cap stocks have earned 11%, according to Ibbotson Associates. If you invest $180 a month over 40 years, that is the difference between more than $200,000 and more than $1.2 million.

How should investors go about selecting an S&P 500 index fund?

Choose the lowest-cost fund. Also check the minimum initial investment required.

What about small-cap or foreign indexes?

There is nothing wrong with investing in other stock market indexes in addition to the S&P 500. But expenses will be higher—because of higher trading costs—and they might not provide the diversification that you expect. Investing in more than one fund also means you would have to rebalance at least once a year to return to your target asset allocation.

Are exchange-traded index derivatives a good idea?

These funds, which include Standard & Poor's Depositary Receipts (SPDRs), have lower annual expenses than index mutual funds, but investors must pay a commission when they purchase shares. If you purchase shares every month, that can add up. In the end, it's probably best to stick with regular index funds.

Is this a bad time to invest in an S&P 500 fund, given the dicey market?

Timing is largely irrelevant. Even professional investors are not good at predicting when to invest. If anything, it's better to start out at a time when the market has been struggling. Since shares are relatively cheap, you'll own more by the time things start turning around.

What about investors who don't have 40 years until retirement?

It is hard to save when time is short. Many people want to become millionaires. If you have 25 years, you'll have to invest $805 a month—instead of $180—assuming a 10% annual return, to reach $1 million by age 65. With 20 years, that jumps to $1,382 a month. With 15 years, it's $2,491. That does *not* mean an S&P 500 index fund isn't the way to go. If you're starting late, you need the big returns that come from stocks.

Shouldn't older investors be more conservative?

If you already have enough to retire on, sure. But if you're nearing retirement and you don't have enough, you can't afford that luxury.

People these days are living so long that they shouldn't expect to retire at 65 and have just five or 10 years in retirement. I'm 62, and my money is still 100% in stocks. When I actually move into my retirement years, I will start to slowly shift some assets into a bond index fund.

■

TOO MUCH DIVERSIFICATION?

Source: **Ralph Acampora, CMT**, managing director, director of technical research, Prudential Securities Inc., One New York Plaza, New York City 10292.

You can't be too diversified in terms of asset allocation—spreading money between stocks, bonds, commodities, real estate, cash, etc. But in the stock portion of your portfolio, as Fidelity's Peter Lynch has said, diversification can become *deworsification* if you buy too many stocks. Then, your portfolio will mirror the market as a whole, and you'd be better off in terms of fees and expenses to buy a broad-based index fund. For an individual stock portfolio, 20 to 25 stocks offers about the right amount of diversification for most investors.

■

EASY WAYS TO CUT TAXES ON INVESTMENT INCOME

Source: **Robert Willens, CPA,** managing director, Lehman Brothers, Inc., 745 Seventh Ave., New York City 10019.

Tax rates are declining, but they're still steep. In 2002 and 2003, the top federal rate on ordinary income is 38.6%. When you add state and local taxes, the top tax rate can reach 45%.

Here are 12 strategies that will reduce the impact of taxes on your investment income...

• ***Don't actively trade your investments—hold them for the long term.*** Active traders have a reportable gain (or loss) each time they buy or sell. This includes exchanging shares within a mutual fund family—the switch involves selling and buying.

WORSE: Trading actively means you can run up very large commissions.

• ***Avoid taking short-term gains.*** Monitor the holding period of your investments so that you own them for more than 12 months before selling. Sell sooner, and you'll have a short-term gain taxed at the top ordinary income tax rate, rather than at a tax-favored long-term gain.

ADVANTAGE: The top tax rate for long-term gains is only 20%—about half the top rate for short-term gains.

CAUTION: Don't hold on to an investment solely for the potential tax benefit—you must keep your investment objectives paramount.

• ***Choose investments that minimize your tax bill.*** An S&P 500 index mutual fund, for example, minimizes taxes by not aggressively trading its holdings.

SOPHISTICATED ALTERNATIVE: Buy a futures or option contract tied to the S&P 500. If you cash out in less than a year and a day, you receive favorable tax treatment. Sixty percent of your profits are considered long-term and 40% short-term, regardless of how long you held the contract.

If you're in the top bracket, your tax rate on such a sale is only 27.44%, rather than 38.6% for pure short-term gain.

• ***Borrow to raise cash rather than selling appreciated shares.*** When you sell shares, you'll pay a substantial part of your profits in taxes.

BETTER: Borrow against these securities from your broker —go on margin. Broker loan rates are now about 6%, and the interest is deductible up to the amount of your investment income for the year.

• ***Buy individual stocks instead of stock mutual funds.*** If you buy and hold a stock, you retain control over its taxation. Your only current tax obligation is from dividends the stock pays, and you can realize gain or loss when it's best for you.

CONTRAST: Mutual fund managers are often forced to sell stocks to generate cash for shareholders who redeem their shares. This can trigger a capital gains distribution, which is taxable even if you reinvest it in additional fund shares.

• ***Select low-turnover/tax-efficient mutual funds.*** If you prefer mutual funds to individual stocks, hunt for a fund with low turnover of its holdings. This will minimize the gains that the fund distributes to you.

Inefficient funds sometimes give up as much as 50% of their returns to taxes. The most tax-efficient funds tend to be those that track an index, since companies are rarely added or deleted. These funds have few forced sales that translate into taxable distributions to investors.

Alternatively, consider actively managed funds that aim for tax efficiency.

EXAMPLE: Vanguard's Tax-Managed Growth and Income Fund (VTGIX). It hasn't distributed a capital gain to shareholders throughout its almost-eight-year existence.

CAUTION: The longer a fund has been managed in a tax-efficient manner, the larger the buildup of its unrealized (embedded) capital gains. This can mean big taxable distributions if the fund is forced to sell shares to finance redemptions.

• ***Buy exchange-traded funds (ETFs).*** As an alternative to tax-efficient mutual funds, you can buy exchange-traded funds. Like stock, these index funds trade on an exchange. There's no need for the fund to sell stocks to meet redemptions—though ETFs can and do make capital gains distributions.

• ***Keep track of dividends and fund distributions you reinvest.*** Include these amounts in the basis (tax cost) of your holding so you don't pay tax on them twice. If you don't do this, you'll pay tax once when the amount is distributed and again when you sell the shares.

• ***Track your purchases.*** When you acquire shares at different times and then sell part of your holding of those shares, you can control your gain or loss.

Do this by identifying for tax purposes which shares, with which basis, you are selling. This is called the "specific identification method."

• ***Track your sales.*** Keep note of all gains you've taken during the year. This will allow you to make tax-advantageous year-end sales, such as selling loss shares to offset realized gains.

Generally, you want to realize $3,000 of capital losses in excess of capital gains each year. You can use this amount to offset salary and other income.

BONUS: Tracking sales helps you avoid the wash-sale rule—a prohibition on reporting any loss if you buy substantially identical securities 30 days before or after the date of sale.

• ***Track investment expenses.*** Investment newspapers, magazines, on-line research fees, etc., are deductible as miscellaneous itemized deductions, to the extent they exceed 2% of adjusted gross income (AGI).

• ***Use investment vehicles that let you defer or avoid tax on gains...***

• Section 529 accounts and Coverdell education savings accounts (ESAs). Funds used for qualified education purposes through these accounts are tax free.

• Tax-deferred annuities. Fixed and variable annuities shelter investment earnings from tax until funds are withdrawn from the account.

• Roth IRAs. Earnings are tax free if contributions are held in the account for at least five years and other conditions are met.

• Traditional IRAs, 401(k) plans and 403(b) annuities. Nothing is taxed until distributions are taken.

CAUTION: In a tax-deferred account, such as a traditional IRA, capital losses can't be used to offset gains. When taking distributions upon retirement, the payout is taxed as ordinary income, even if the money was generated by capital gains.

HOLDING STRATEGY: Shelter investments that produce ordinary income—such as bonds—in tax-deferred retirement accounts. Hold investments producing capital gains in taxable accounts. This may align your portfolio better for tax efficiency. ■

ANTIQUE STOCK & BOND CERTIFICATES

Source: **Malcolm Katt,** an antiques dealer and owner of Millwood Gallery, Box 552, Millwood, New York 10546.

Stock and bond certificates issued by corporations and governments in years gone by are valuable collectors' items. Yet the market for them is still new enough for collectors to get in on the ground floor.

OPPORTUNITY: Unlike the mature markets of stamp and coin collecting, most collectors of financial certificates are still focused on building collections rather than selling them.

Attractive collections can be put together with a little legwork and research, and should rise in value quickly as the number of bidding collectors grows.

EXAMPLE: There was no auction market in the US for such certificates until 1980. But last year, top prices for individual certificates at auction broke the $100,000 level.

ATTRACTIONS: Stock and bond certificates often are exceptional artworks designed by notable engravers and artists.

Many certificates open a window on history by having been associated with famous events or signed by famous people—including businessmen such as John D. Rockefeller, Walt Disney and Thomas Edison, as well as political leaders of earlier eras, even kings.

Because much less research has been done by collectors of financial certificates than by stamp and coin collectors, new collectors have a real chance to make important and valuable discoveries.

Anyone can start a collection by purchasing certificates for as little as $10 each.

HELP GETTING STARTED: The International Bond & Share Society, 15 Dyatt Pl., Box 430, Hackensack, New Jersey 07602, *www.scripophily.org.*

■

BEST INVESTMENTS FOR OUR CHANGED WORLD

Source: **Allen Sinai, PhD,** founder, chief global economist/strategist and president of Decision Economics, Inc., an economic and financial information support and advisory firm with offices in New York, Boston, London and Tokyo. *www.pde.primark.com.* Before starting Decision Economics in 1996, Dr. Sinai was chief global economist and managing director at Lehman Brothers and director of Lehman Brothers Global Economics.

The investment picture, which had been murky in the immediate aftermath of September 11, 2001, is finally coming into clearer focus. The US economy is likely to move gradually, and irregularly, from recession to slow growth to expansion.

Most investment decisions should be based on what the economy will be doing one to three years hence. By 2004, and perhaps by the second half of 2003, the economy should be healthy again, growing by more than 3% a year.

ECONOMIC POSITIVES...

• ***Low short-term interest rates.*** Low interest rates make stocks more attractive because of higher valuations and reduce the cost-of-capital to business, which helps business spending. Rates are unlikely to rise before mid-2003.

• ***Lower taxes.*** Another $40 billion in tax cuts from the Bush Administration's 10-year, $1.35 trillion tax-cut program. This helps consumer spending. Even more tax cuts will be proposed and probably passed in 2003.

• ***Higher government spending*** to fight terrorism and help revive the economy.

• ***Even lower inflation.*** A drop in the inflation rate from more than 2% in 2001 to near 1%. This will help the purchasing power of consumers and businesses.

• ***Strong productivity growth.*** A source of increased demand and supply that can help grow the economy.

STOCK MARKET STRATEGY...

The market has been falling based on uncertainties over the economic recovery, business profits and geopolitical risks. But over this next year we should enter a sustained, but choppy, upturn in stock prices. A year from now, the Dow

Jones Industrial Average (DJIA) will be trading at higher levels. Some new monies can go into stocks now on this prospect.

Of course, further terrorist attacks and a drawn-out war with Iraq could derail the recovery and cause a correction in the market.

My asset allocation now is 50% equities...42% bonds...8% cash or money market funds. When I am neutral—neither bullish nor bearish—on the stock market, I keep 55% in stocks. This equity allocation should move higher in coming months.

I like large companies with proven track records that are well positioned to withstand another global recession and that will over time benefit from a US upturn. Many stocks in the DJIA and large, nontechnology companies in the Standard & Poor's 500 stock index fit the bill.

FAVORITE SECTORS...

- ***Health care.*** Stocks of drug/pharmaceutical companies are more resistant to economic ups and downs. Demand for their products will remain strong because of aging demographics and product innovations.
- ***Financials.*** I like stocks of banks, investment banks and brokerage firms. But be selective. Emphasize companies that have more than one revenue stream and are good at managing credit risk. More credit problems are likely to surface, hurting some financial companies.
- ***Consumer staples.*** I prefer companies that make items people *must* buy in the US and elsewhere—such as food and household products.
- ***Utilities.*** Electric companies are still safe havens. People must have electric power. Look for utilities whose financials are strong enough to support the current dividend, with service areas prosperous enough to ride out a new recession. Dividend yields tend to be high for these firms and investors can't get high cash returns anywhere else now.

SECTORS TO AVOID...

- ***Energy.*** Despite OPEC's efforts to further curtail production, oil is a commodity, and commodity prices inevitably fall or stay low in a weak global economy. Crude oil prices have an Iraq war premium in them that could go away.

• *Airlines.* This is a devastating time for the airline business. In two to three years, airlines could turn around, but it's far too early to consider these stocks now.

• *Technology.* I expect the technology sector to be a solid place to invest over the next three years. But near-term, technology is risky. Any corrections in the overall stock market will pummel volatile sectors, particularly technology. Don't shift into technology or other high-growth sectors until the economy has high odds of regaining its footing.

■

REBALANCING ACT

Source: **John Markese,** president, American Association of Individual Investors, Chicago, *www.aaii.com.*

Rebalancing your portfolio? Do it with new money you have to invest rather than incurring capital gains or losses by selling what you already have. It's valid to sell for performance reasons, but not simply to adjust the balance of stocks and bonds in your holdings. If, say, bonds have outgrown your chosen asset allocation for fixed income, put new money into stocks until your portfolio is back in balance.

■

INVESTMENT WISDOM

Source: **Suze Orman, CFP,** lecturer and author of *The Courage to Be Rich: Creating a Life of Material and Spiritual Abundance.* Riverhead.

Leave your investments untouched for at least six months following a divorce or the death of your spouse. Emotionally draining experiences leave you ill-prepared to make key decisions about investing your money or entrusting it to someone else to invest.

BETTER: Leave savings in a safe place until your emotional equilibrium and sound judgment return.

■

A GOOD READ

Source: **Ellen Hoffman,** retirement columnist in Shepherdstown, West Virginia, *www.retirementcatchup.com.* She is author of *The Retirement Catch-Up Guide.* Newmarket.

Read all investment statements. Monthly and annual statements can be a chore to read and understand. But people and computers make mistakes. It's your money—you need to keep a close watch on it. Even if you use a financial adviser, talk with him/her regularly—and keep track of your own investments. ■

SAVING MONEY

THE COUPON QUEEN HELPS YOU SAVE MONEY EVERY DAY

Source: **Ellie Kay,** the "Coupon Queen," a writer in Alamogordo, New Mexico, *www.elliekay.com.* Her latest book is *How to Save Money Every Day.* Bethany House.

When my husband and I got married, between us we were $40,000 in debt.

We resolved to make whatever lifestyle changes were necessary to get out from under. To do this, we found ways to live on less than 25% of one income. Within two years, we were free of debt, despite donating 10% of our income to charity.

Here are some of our secrets for significantly cutting costs...

FOOD...

- ***Coupons.*** Every true penny-pincher clips coupons. *Also:* Search the manufacturer's Web site for coupon offers there.

TWICE AS GOOD: Double coupons. If your supermarket does not offer them, get friends to sign a petition saying they would patronize the store more often if it offered double coupons.

Show this to the store manager. If he/she is reluctant, suggest that he try offering double coupons only on the slowest day of the week—and see if sales increase.

• ***Milk, meat and produce.*** Coupons are seldom available for these staples, but you can save by buying when they are on sale.

Stock up on meat specials and freeze...and take advantage of stores that match prices offered in competitors' ads. Many Wal-Mart superstores will do this.

To save on fruit and vegetables, get to know the people who set them out in the store. Ask for a discount on imperfect produce. You may have to cut out some bruises, but what's left is perfectly good.

EVEN BETTER: If you live close to a wholesale produce supplier, its rejects are apt to be in better shape than those available at the retailer.

• ***Food co-ops.*** If you get 10 people together who make a regular monthly order, you can form a co-op to buy produce from a wholesaler. Members must pay up front and always take their order—or find someone else to take it.

FURNITURE AND APPLIANCES...

Before buying furniture, ask yourself: "Do I need it? Can I afford it? How am I going to pay for it?"

Write down your dream list, and take it to a furniture store. Compare the amount of cash you have to spend with the cost of what you want to buy. Factor in the interest you will pay if you buy on credit.

EXAMPLE: The new furniture you want costs $10,000 more than you have in cash. Suppose you use store credit to pay for it. If you make the monthly minimum payment at typical interest rates of 18% to 22%, your new furniture will end up costing you $26,000. It would take you more than 33 years to pay off that debt.

Here are some alternatives...

• ***The Internet.*** Many furniture manufacturers list outlet stores on their Web sites. Search for the price of the pieces you want. Go back to the store and ask if it can match the prices.

Or print out a list of all the furniture distributors within a 100-mile radius. Call them and ask for their best price. Then go back to your local store and give it a chance to match it.

Finally, ask if it can *beat* that price by throwing in free delivery, free fabric treatment, etc.

POTENTIAL SAVINGS: Up to 50%.

• ***Furniture craftsmen.*** Local craftsmen often build custom furniture for less than the retail price. Locate craftsmen by asking at local lumberyards, antique stores and furniture repair shops...or look in the *Yellow Pages* under "Custom Builders" and "Furniture Designers."

Before calling for an estimate, make sure that you know exactly what you want in terms of type and quality of wood, style, finish, fabric and price range. Ask whether the craftsman can suggest a less costly alternative.

• ***Model homes.*** Call local builders. Make an offer for furniture and appliances in their model homes.

CAUTION: The furniture displayed in model homes is usually smaller than regular furniture—to make the homes appear bigger to prospective purchasers.

• ***Floor models.*** Some appliance dealers and department stores sell floor models at a discount. These appliances usually still carry a new appliance guarantee. If they have minor cosmetic damage, you may be able to reduce the price even more.

• ***Secondhand merchandise.*** Check out local secondhand stores, garage sales and classified ads for quality merchandise. Inspect old furniture for quality and condition.

Check ads for used merchandise on bulletin boards in supermarkets, libraries, churches and workplaces—and post your own ad specifying what you are looking for.

ENTERTAINMENT AND TRAVEL...

• ***Zoos and museums.*** A family membership to your local zoo or museum may allow you to visit similar institutions all over the country—free of charge.

• ***Travel savings.*** The best place to look for travel bargains is on the Internet. Visit *www.bestfares.com, www.cheaptickets.com, www.smarterliving.com* or *www.expedia.com* (also at 800-397-3342). Try the airlines directly for specials on their own Web sites. Search for hotel rate specials at *www.travelweb.com* ...or make an offer at *www.priceline.com.* If your Priceline bid is accepted, you must pay for it whether you go or not.

■

HOW TO GET THE BEST BARGAINS ON THE PLANET

Source: **Kathy Borrus,** Washington, DC–based author of *The Fearless Shopper: How to Get the Best Deals on the Planet.* Travelers Tales. She is the former merchandise manager for the Smithsonian Institution Museum Shops and is now a specialty retail marketing consultant.

Whether you're planning to shop at the many flea markets in Paris or at the bazaars in Morocco, the strategies I learned as a buyer for the Smithsonian Institution Museum Shops will help you score real finds.

GROUND RULES...

Before leaving home, take the time to prepare for shopping in a foreign country.

- ***Learn from guidebooks or the Internet about the customs,*** regional specialties and indigenous arts and crafts of the country.
- ***Focus your shopping activities by knowing before you travel...***
- What you'd like to buy.
- For whom you are buying.
- How much you can spend.
- ***Take along small tokens from home,*** such as pens, T-shirts and caps. Use them for barter or to negotiate a better price.
- ***Comparison shop before you leave home.*** If the country you're visiting has a reputation for good prices on certain items, check out prices on similar items at home. Write down those prices and take them with you.
- ***Bring along a calculator or create a "cheat sheet" of the currency rates,*** especially if you're bargaining in a foreign language.
- ***Learn about a foreign country's entry and exit requirements for goods.*** In some countries, buying art and antiques may require an export license, which could result in unexpected duties or fees. **EXAMPLES...**
- Egyptian law prohibits exportation of items more than 100 years old.
- In Laos, you can't take antiques or representations of Buddha out of the country.

• In Russia, you need permission from the Ministry of Culture to export anything made before 1945. Exportation of antique icons is strictly forbidden.

• In South and Central America, the export of pre-Columbian artifacts is prohibited in most areas—check with the country you will be visiting to verify what their rules are.

FLEA MARKETS AND ANTIQUE FAIRS...

• ***Pay in cash***—it gives you better bargaining leverage.

• ***Act like a seasoned buyer***—always ask the price first and negotiate from there.

• ***Unless you can tell the difference between a fake and something authentic, don't buy it.*** Forgeries abound—especially in bronze castings, coins and old drawings. Watch for fake jade in China and Hong Kong.

• ***Be informed about prices***—carry a price guide for antiques.

• ***Bargain politely***—express a willingness to buy at the right price and keep the negotiations friendly. Ask questions like, "Is this your best price?" or "Can you do better?" Or say, "I don't usually pay that much for this type of item."

• ***Dress down when shopping at an open-air market.*** Leave your jewelry and expensive outfits home.

BAZAARS, SOUKS AND MARKETS...

Win the bargaining game using these strategies...

• ***Get a feel for the market***—look around before you buy.

• ***Shop with a native if possible***—you'll get better deals. Alternatively, learn as many key phrases and numbers in the language. Learn to say "too much" and "what's the cost?"

• ***Visit individual villages away from major cities.*** You can often buy folk crafts directly from the artisans—prices will usually be lower and the quality better.

• ***Bargain in a spirit of fun and friendliness.*** *Always* reject the first offer.

• ***Bring cash***—most merchants won't accept credit cards. You're usually in a better position if you have local currency (although in some places, US dollars are desirable). Keep small bills handy.

BECOME A FEARLESS BARGAINER...

Merchants know just where the profit margins are and what they can afford. Here's how to negotiate the best deal—even when prices are already low...

• ***Before you bargain, decide what the item is worth to you.*** Then ask the price—that way you'll know how much bargaining room you have.

• ***See what the locals are buying and how much they're paying.***

• ***If a merchant asks an absurdly high price, offer an equally ridiculous low price***—you'll probably meet somewhere in the middle. Don't be afraid to make an offer—all anyone can say is no.

• ***Be willing to walk away***—you can often get what you want if you're not attached to it. Stick to your budget and your lists.

If you're uncomfortable with the bargaining process, look for state-run cooperatives and handcraft cooperatives—they generally offer indigenous items for sale at reasonable prices.

COMING HOME...

You're usually better off carrying your items home in your checked luggage than shipping them. Before buying items that will have to be shipped, factor in the shipping cost. It's no bargain to buy a $300 wooden chest in New Delhi if it costs another $300 to send it home.

The value-added tax (VAT)—the European version of a sales tax—is always included in the price of an item. Foreigners are exempt from the VAT and entitled to a refund. But getting the refund can be a hassle. You need receipts and must wait in designated customs lines at the airport.

Learn country-specific VAT regulations at *www.taxfree.se.*

US Customs lets you bring $400 worth of goods back to the US duty free. Above that, you pay a 10% duty tax on up to $1,000 of goods. Remember—you can't bring into the US any item made of ivory or turtle shell.

Get a free copy of the pamphlet "Know Before You Go" from the US Customs Service at *www.customs.gov/travel/travel.htm.*

■

SHREWD WAYS TO PROTECT YOUR ASSETS AGAINST A LAWSUIT

Source: **Gideon Rothschild, Esq., CPA,** partner in the law firm Moses & Singer LLP, 1301 Avenue of the Americas, New York City 10019. *www.mosessinger.com.*

We really do live in a litigious society. Even if you've done nothing wrong, you can find yourself the target of a ruinous lawsuit. But if you act *before* anyone sues, you can protect your assets. The sooner you act, the more options you have.

YOUR HOLDINGS...

Look to see where you are most vulnerable to a lawsuit. These areas should be the focus of your asset-protection plans. **CONSIDER...**

• ***Your business interests.*** To what extent are your personal assets vulnerable as a result of your owning and/or running a business? Have you personally guaranteed any of your corporation's debts?

STRATEGY: If you are a general partner of a business, consider transforming that ownership interest into a limited liability company (LLC). Having the LLC act as the general partner will protect your personal assets.

• ***Your personal life.*** To what extent are you personally vulnerable as a result of your marital status? If you are married, what impact would divorce have on your assets? Be sure to consider state property rights (such as community property), prenuptial agreements and any other arrangements you might have made.

BEWARE: The wealthier you are, the more vulnerable you are to personal lawsuits arising from car accidents and injuries that occur on your property.

YOUR INSURANCE...

Insurance is your first line of defense against a lawsuit. *Two reasons:* The policy will pay off if you're found liable. And the insurance company may be required to defend you—saving you costly legal fees.

Review the policies you now hold. Make sure you're covered for every future legal action you may be exposed to. **KEY POLICIES TO HAVE...**

• *Umbrella policy.* It supplements the coverage under your homeowner's and car insurance policies. Such a policy typically provides an additional $1 million to $10 million in coverage. The greater your personal wealth, the bigger your umbrella policy should be.

• *D&O coverage.* If you are a corporate director or officer—or a member of the board of directors of a nonprofit organization—make sure you're covered for actions against directors and officers. Ask to see a copy of the policy before agreeing to serve in such positions.

• *Malpractice insurance.* If you are a doctor, lawyer or other professional who may be the object of a malpractice suit, make sure you understand the extent of your policy's coverage—the types of legal actions it will and will not cover.

CHANGE OF OWNERSHIP...

How are your assets owned? The way you hold title to property can make it less vulnerable to creditors' claims. **CONSIDER THESE CHANGES...**

• *Transfer assets to your spouse or children.* Assuming the transfers are made before a problem arises, this strategy should fully protect the assets.

• *Change title of jointly owned assets into "tenancy by the entirety."* When real estate is held in tenancy by the entirety, the creditors of one spouse cannot get at the assets of the other.

In a few states (such as Florida, Pennsylvania and Virginia), tenancy by the entirety can be used for more than just real estate. In those states, it can, for instance, be used to protect brokerage accounts.

• *Create family limited partnerships to own securities.* While this strategy does not fully protect the holdings, it makes it more difficult for creditors to reach them.

ALTERNATIVE: Set up a charitable remainder trust to own the securities. You can receive an income for life from the trust, with the assets then passing to the charity. Tax-wise, you obtain an immediate income tax deduction for the value of the charity's remainder interest.

For asset protection purposes, creditors may be able to reach your income interest in a charitable remainder trust—but probably only for a limited number of years (typically a judgment runs for 10 years). If this happens, you will at least have protected the remaining years of income and all of the underlying trust assets.

- ***Set up a limited liability company to own any real estate now held in your name.*** Then, if any legal action arises from the real estate, your personal assets will be protected.

BANKRUPTCY EXEMPTIONS...

Federal and state bankruptcy laws let you protect certain assets from creditors—even if your financial situation is so dire that you must file for bankruptcy.

- ***Homestead protection.*** Most states provide some protection from creditors for the equity in your home. A handful of states provide generous protection. Florida, for example, completely exempts a home from creditors' claims—even if it's purchased on the eve of bankruptcy.

- ***Retirement plans and IRAs.*** Federal law exempts assets in qualified retirement plans from creditors' claims. The extent of asset protection for IRAs and other non-qualified plans (including Roth IRAs) varies from state to state. For a listing by state of exemptions available, visit *www.mosessinger.com/resources/protecting.shtml.*

- ***Annuities and life insurance.*** Some degree of protection is offered in some states. Check state law. For a listing by state of exemptions available, visit *www.mosessinger.com/resources/creditprotec.shtml.*

NOTE: Federal bankruptcy reform, which failed to be enacted last summer, would have limited some exemptions—such as complete homestead exemptions. It remains to be seen whether Congress will again take up bankruptcy reform. For a listing of state exemptions, visit the above Web site.

ASSET PROTECTION TRUST...

Asset protection trusts are designed to give you unfettered access to your funds while protecting them from creditors' claims. The trusts are "self-settled," meaning you set them up with your own assets, and you remain as beneficiary.

IMPORTANT: Asset protection trusts do *not* provide tax savings...

• ***For income tax purposes***—since you continue to be the "owner" of the trust, you are taxed on trust earnings.

• ***For estate tax purposes***—unless the transfer is treated as a completed gift subject to gift tax, the assets must be included in your taxable estate.

• ***Domestic asset protection trusts.*** Asset protection trusts—in which you are both the grantor (or "settlor") and the beneficiary—can now be set up in Alaska, Delaware, Nevada and Rhode Island. (Colorado also allows self-settled "spendthrift trusts," but does not provide as broad protection for settlors as the other four states.) Unlike other self-settled trusts, state law in these jurisdictions provides protection for these trusts.

How much protection do they offer? Residents of these states can obtain protection for assets held in these trusts. It is not clear, however, whether nonresidents can achieve the same asset protection by setting up a trust in one of these states. For example, it is unclear whether a New York resident who sets up a Delaware asset protection trust will have his assets fully protected in case of court action arising in New York.

• ***Offshore asset protection trusts.*** Two dozen foreign jurisdictions cater to Americans who want to set up asset protection trusts. The most popular sites now being used—Cook Islands, Nevis, St. Lucia and St. Vincent.

CAUTION: Beware of offshore trust scams promising asset protection and no federal income taxes. At *www.irs.gov,* the IRS lists scams it has uncovered. The Financial & Tax Fraud Education Associates, Inc. Web site, *www.quatloos.com,* lists what it considers offshore scams to avoid.

■

HOW TO CUT CREDIT CARD COSTS

Source: **Rob** and **Terry Adams,** longtime bargain hunters in Panama City Beach, Florida, and authors of *The Bargain Hunter's Field Guide.* Avebury.

• ***When offered a low interest rate, check how long it lasts***—many run for only a few months.

• ***Look for a grace period—without any interest***—for making payments.

• ***If a card offer includes special features,*** such as no annual fee or a low fixed rate, find out if your current cards already offer them—many issuers have the same enhancements.

• ***If a new offer really is better, call your current issuer*** and ask it to match the offer.

■

BUSINESS SMARTS

BOOTSTRAPPING—HOW TO START A BUSINESS FOR $1,000 OR LESS

Source: **Barbara Weltman, Esq.,** author of many books on small business, including *J.K. Lasser's New Rules for Small Business Taxes.* John Wiley & Sons. She is editor/publisher of *Barbara Weltman's Big Ideas for Small Business,* a monthly newsletter. *www.bwideas.com.*

Bootstrapping involves starting a business with whatever cash you can scrape together. Hewlett-Packard, United Parcel Service and Walt Disney all began as bootstrap ventures that grew into global giants. You may not have your sights set that high. But for $1,000 or less, you can bootstrap a postretirement business that will keep you occupied *and* produce enough cash to secure your senior years.

The current global slowdown might be reason enough to postpone launching a more ambitious business. But bootstrap operations typically serve a niche. And a niche business, if it delivers the right product or service at the right price, can thrive in any economic climate.

Here's how to bootstrap a retirement business…

• ***Stick to what you know best.*** The first impulse of many retirees is to buy an existing business or become a franchisee. Either approach will cost many thousands of dollars and most likely put you into a field where you have no experience. Odds are great that you'll lose your investment.

BEST STRATEGY: Carve out a niche in the industry where you have the most experience. Think through products and/or services that would benefit someone in your industry, but that aren't available at a reasonable price.

EXAMPLES: If you're in sales, sell to businesses too small to warrant the attention of the full-time sales staff of larger businesses. If you're in marketing, serve your old employer and others in your industry on an outsource basis. With your low overhead, you can profit where bigger ventures could not.

• ***Keep costs under control.*** Start with as little of your own capital as possible and with no borrowed money. Gambling your time on the business is one thing. Gambling your retirement savings is something else.

I'm assuming you'll run the business from your home and that you already own a computer. **IF SO, EXPECT TO FACE THESE EXPENSES…**

• Raw materials. If you're launching a service business, you'll need only a second phone line and office supplies. If launching a product-based business, you'll need to invest in materials. Keep initial purchases to a minimum—letting inventory build up only as sales build up.

• Professional fees. Whoever does your taxes can handle what additional work the business generates at little or no added expense. You probably won't need an accountant until the business is much bigger.

Whether you need a lawyer depends on the form your business takes. You can launch a sole proprietorship without legal help. The main drawback to a sole proprietorship is that your personal assets are exposed to claims against the business.

You can shield personal assets by incorporating or forming a limited liability company. Setup will cost \$300 to \$600 in legal fees. But you can do it yourself for less (for instance at *www.bizfilings.com*).

• Start-up costs. Whatever your business, keep start-up costs to $1,000 or less. Finance growth from business profits. That's what bootstrapping is all about.

• ***Set out to make profits.*** Some people form a retirement business simply to fill their days. You can find cheaper ways of killing time than starting a business. Start the business only if careful analysis tells you it has the potential of making money.

TIME LINE: Don't expect to make money immediately. You'll have start-up costs and a learning curve to get past. It will take time to make yourself known to customers.

If you can't see yourself turning a profit within two years, don't start the business. If you're not making money within two years of starting the business, think about folding it.

The more your bootstrap business relies on skills developed during your working life, the more likely you are to make money. If you spent your life in public relations, for instance, your best chance for profits is by drawing on your contacts in public relations.

• ***Understand the effort involved in running a business.*** When you're running your own business, you must handle *everything*—from sales and marketing to accounting and collections. I find that most people are unprepared for the time running a new business takes and the diversity of responsibilities they must take on.

EXAMPLE: One couple thought their hobby of collecting antiques would make it easy to launch a business selling antiques on-line. They learned the hard way how much time it takes to photograph each item, write the description, post it to the auction site, pack and ship the item and follow up to get paid for the sale.

Don't assume you can start a new business as a hobby, to be worked at part-time and halfheartedly. To make your venture work, you need the same commitment and passion any entrepreneur brings to a start-up.

• ***Get your business noticed.*** The cheapest way is word of mouth. If you're in the same field as you were in your pre-retirement years, hit your Rolodex and let people know you're out there.

Do you need a Web site? A Web site can put a small local venture on equal footing with a global giant. But creating and maintaining a Web site takes time and money. Most start-ups *don't* need one.

• ***Avoid the pitfalls that sink new businesses.*** The biggest problem for most start-ups is not having a clear focus on what the business will do and what the founder will get out of it.

Every business needs a business plan—even if the business is a bootstrap operation that will never grow very large.

The plan should describe the business in detail, how much it will cost to get started and where you expect the business to be in one, three and five years.

Draw up a budget for what it will cost you to get going and how much more it will cost you each month until you become profitable.

For help in crafting a business plan, turn to the Small Business Administration *(www.sba.gov).* You'll find a wealth of information about starting businesses. For most bootstrap businesses, the SBA site will provide all the start-up help you need—at no cost.

■

S CORPORATION BENEFITS

Source: **Martin S. Kaplan, CPA,** partner, Geller, Marzano & Co., CPAs, 225 W. 34 St., New York City 10122.

Business proprietors can reduce both taxes and audit risk by converting their businesses to S corporations.

Taxes can be reduced because all of a proprietor's income reported on Schedule C is subject to self-employment tax of 15.3%. But only the salary that an S corporation pays its owner/employee is subject to employment tax—since profit after reasonable salary is paid is free from employment tax.

Audit risk is reduced because business deductions taken by individuals on Schedule C are scrutinized by the IRS—and these "audit flags" are removed when the deductions are taken instead on an S corporation's return. Also, S corporation returns are audited much less frequently than proprietors' returns.

■

BIG TAX-SAVING IDEAS FOR SMALL-BUSINESS OWNERS

Source: **Barbara Weltman, Esq.,** author of many books on small business, including *J.K. Lasser's New Rules for Small Business Taxes.* John Wiley & Sons. She is editor/publisher of *Barbara Weltman's Big Ideas for Small Business,* a monthly newsletter. *www.bwideas.com.*

Your bottom line—profits after tax—is the measure of the success of your business. Achieving success depends to a great extent on your understanding of the tax law. Only when you understand the law can you take advantage of the many opportunities for tax saving—and avoid the pitfalls. **BASICS...**

The way you set up your business—that is, the legal form of your business—affects...

- ***The tax rates you'll pay on profits.***
- ***Who pays employment taxes and on what income.***
- ***The fringe benefits you can receive tax free.***

TAX RATES ON PROFITS...

- ***Sole proprietorships, partnerships, limited liability companies (LLCs) and S corporations.*** With these "pass-through entities" owners pay tax on their share of business profits at their individual tax rates.

The income tax on the profits passed through to these owners can be as high as 38.6% in 2002 and 2003. Two owners in the same company may be paying a different rate on the same share of profits if they are in different individual tax brackets.

- ***C corporations.*** They pay graduated tax rates ranging from 15% to 35%.
- ***Personal service corporations.*** C corporations engaged in the fields of health, law, accounting, engineering, architecture, actuarial science, performing arts or consulting, and that meet certain ownership and service tests, pay a flat tax of 35%.

TREATMENT OF LOSSES...

Owners of pass-through entities can use their share of business losses to offset their income from other sources on their personal returns—subject to certain limitations.

EXAMPLE: If a consultant operating as a sole proprietor has a net business loss of $15,000, he/she can use this loss to offset a spouse's salary, interest and dividend income—as well as gains from sales of stocks or other property.

Owners of C corporations do not directly benefit from business losses—such losses offset only corporate income on the corporate return.

FRINGE BENEFITS...

The tax law provides a number of benefits that can be offered to employees on a tax-free basis.

The business deducts the cost of providing the benefits. The net result is greater after-tax income to the owners.

However, except for retirement plans that can be used by all types of businesses, other fringe benefits generally cannot be provided tax free to owners of pass-through entities. Only C corporation owners can benefit from these tax-free perks.

STRATEGY: Start-ups may want to use pass-through entities so that owners can use business losses on their personal returns. But once a business becomes profitable, it may be wise to become a C corporation so that owners can benefit from tax-free fringes that the business can now afford to provide.

EMPLOYMENT TAXES...

Self-employed individuals, including general partners and LLC members, pay self-employment tax (which is both the employer and employee share of FICA) on net earnings from self-employment. Half of this tax is deductible.

For partners and LLC members, net income from self-employment generally means their share of the business's net income, whether distributed or not. So, these owners pay self-employment tax on earnings they may not have received.

In contrast, shareholders (whether in a C or an S corporation) pay the employee share of FICA only on their salary—and the corporation pays the employer share as well.

CAUTION: It is not clear when LLC members can be treated as limited partners exempt from self-employment tax.

NAILING DOWN DEDUCTIONS...

Business owners know that virtually all expenses produce a tax benefit—a deduction or a credit. But the benefit can be lost without records to back up the expenses.

• ***Travel and entertainment costs.*** Generally, owners must keep two types of records—a *diary* or *log* noting certain information ...and *documentary evidence* (canceled checks, receipts, etc.).

The tax law is specific about the type of information to be noted—the amount of the expense, the date it was incurred, the business purpose for the expense and other information dependent upon the nature of the expense. Receipts are not required for an expense (other than lodging) if the amount is less than $75.

STRATEGY: Set up record-keeping policies for owners and employees to follow. Consider using per diem reimbursements for travel and meal expenses to avoid the need to track the amount of the expenses.

• ***Charitable contributions.*** If a business donates $250 or more at one time, a canceled check is not sufficient evidence to support a deduction. There must be an acknowledgment from the charity. If the business donates property, an appraisal may be required.

STRATEGY: C corporations that donate unused inventory to a public charity or an operating foundation for care of the ill, needy or infants, can receive a larger charitable contribution deduction. They can increase the regular deduction, generally limited to cost, by 50% of the difference between cost and the value of the inventory (but not more than 200% of cost).

Special rules also apply to donations of scientific equipment and computers donated to schools and libraries.

• ***Carryovers.*** Many tax write-offs are limited for the current year. However, excess amounts may be carried forward—sometimes for a set number of years, sometimes indefinitely. It's important to keep track of carryovers so they are not overlooked. Common business carryovers for which good records should be maintained...

- Net operating losses.
- Capital losses.
- Charitable contributions.
- Home-office deductions.
- At-risk losses.
- Passive activity losses.

STRATEGY: Review carryovers annually looking for those that are about to expire. This will allow time to plan to use up the carryover.

EXAMPLE: If a corporation's capital loss carryover is about to expire, consider selling property that will produce capital gains to offset the loss. Proceeds can be used to upgrade equipment at no tax cost.

Carryovers aren't the only types of deductions that run beyond the year in which the expense was incurred. Records must be kept for depreciation, the basis of assets (so gains or losses can be figured) and prepaid expenses (insurance, subscriptions, interest and rent).

NEW OPPORTUNITIES...

• ***Credit for retirement plan start-up costs.*** If your business doesn't yet have a qualified retirement plan, you can claim a tax credit for starting one. The credit is 50% of costs, up to a top credit of $500 per year for the first three years of the plan. Only companies with no more than 100 employees qualify for this break.

• ***The first-year expense deduction*** for equipment placed in service in 2002 is $24,000 (in 2003, it's $25,000).

Plan equipment purchases, such as computer upgrades, to take full advantage of this immediate write-off. Equipment purchases in excess of the limit can be depreciated.

• ***The health insurance deduction*** for self-employed individuals is 70% of premiums (in 2003, it's 100%).

Health insurance includes the cost of long-term-care coverage (up to a dollar limit based on current age).

• ***Contributions to SIMPLEs*** (savings incentive match plans for employees) are higher in 2002. The employee salary reduction limit is $7,000 (or $7,500 for someone age 50 or older by the end of 2002), regardless of age. In 2003, the salary reduction amount is $8,000 (or $9,000 for someone age 50 or older by the end of 2003). Higher employee contributions means higher employer matching contributions.

■

BEST WAYS TO USE THE WEALTH IN A FAMILY BUSINESS

Source: **Steven Bandini, CPA,** tax manager, Eisner LLP, 750 Third Ave., New York City 10017.

It's not enough simply to *create* wealth in a business. You want to *use* it in the most tax-advantageous way possible.

Here are six smart business-management strategies that will better enable you to use the wealth for your family's welfare...

• ***Take full advantage of new retirement plan options.*** Recent law changes substantially increase the potential value of qualified retirement plans to private businesses—by increasing contribution limits and loosening prior restrictions.

EXAMPLE: Many private businesses not organized as regular C corporations have self-employed retirement plans. **NEW...**

• Defined-contribution plans can now accept contributions of up to $40,000 per recipient for 2002 and 2003. That figure is up from $35,000 in 2001.

• Owners of self-employed plans can now borrow from them.

• Now only one plan is needed to make a full 25%-of-compensation contribution. Formerly, two plans were needed—a profit-sharing plan to accept up to 15% of compensation plus a money purchase plan to which a fixed amount of compensation (typically 10%) had to be contributed annually.

Allowing the full 25% to be contributed to a profit-sharing plan eliminates the cost of setting up two plans. It also provides for more financial flexibility because the amount contributed to a profit-sharing plan is voluntary and can vary each year.

CAUTION: Those who already have both plans and want to consolidate them should consult a benefits expert before making any changes.

Other kinds of qualified retirement plans similarly benefit from the new law. No matter what kind of plan your business has, review the rule changes with an expert to make the most of them.

EXTRA PAYOFF: Qualified retirement plans protect assets against creditor claims. So they can protect a business owner's personal wealth from the business's creditors should business difficulties arise.

• ***Own business assets separately.*** If assets such as real estate or valuable equipment are used in the business, it may be more advantageous for the business owners to own the assets *separately,* either through an LLC, a partnership or an S corporation, and lease them to the business. **ADVANTAGES...**

• Lease payments for rental real estate provide cash flow from the business to the asset owners without being subject to employment taxes as salary would be. The payments may be sheltered from income tax by depreciation deductions taken for the assets. And the business can deduct the lease payments.

• The owners will be able to sell or finance them in the future to meet their personal needs—rather than have the business own them and receive the proceeds of any sale or financing.

• Assets can be owned in different proportion to shares in the business, as best fits certain family circumstances.

EXAMPLE 1: Assets can be owned by younger family members to shift wealth to them—and to shift lease payments into lower income tax brackets—while older family members retain ownership of the business.

EXAMPLE 2: A family member who is not active in the business may own an asset that is leased to it. The family member receives a share of family wealth and secure income through the lease payments.

• Property not owned by the business is not subject to legal claims that may arise against the firm. So separate ownership of business assets helps protect wealth against the potential claims of business creditors.

• ***Organize the business as a pass-through entity.*** S corporations, limited liability companies (LLCs) and limited partnerships (LPs)—known as pass-through entities—offer tax-planning opportunities that are unavailable through a regular (C) corporation. **THE OPPORTUNITIES INCLUDE...**

• No double tax. Pass-through entities generally aren't subject to corporate income tax. So the potential double taxation of business profits—first as income to the business, then as income to shareholders when distributed to them through dividends—is avoided.

• Income shifting. The income of a pass-through entity is taxed directly on the tax returns of its owners. The tax rate owed on business income may be reduced by giving shares in the firm to low-tax-bracket family members (such as children over age 13).

• Loss shifting. Losses of a pass-through entity are reported on the tax returns of its owners. If certain requirements are met, these losses may be deducted against ordinary income. So a business incurring tax losses—perhaps during the initial years—may serve as a tax shelter for its owners.

STRATEGY: If a business has already been established as a regular (C) corporation and can't change, consider organizing its future expansion through separate pass-through entities.

• ***Hire children in the business.*** A fine way to save taxes is for the business to deduct at a high tax rate salaries paid to children who are in a low tax bracket.

The standard deduction lets a child earn up to $4,700 of wages free from income tax in 2002 ($4,750 in 2003). For three children, that's more than $14,000 of wages income tax free. (Check Social Security tax rules to see if they apply.)

In addition, their salaries will enable the children to fund Roth IRAs that may provide decades of tax-free investment returns for them.

TO MINIMIZE AUDIT RISK: Be sure children are paid a reasonable wage for work they really do.

• ***Maximize fringe benefits.*** This is one area where regular (C) corporations retain an advantage over pass-through entities—they provide for a wider range of tax-favored fringe benefits to their owners.

EXAMPLES: Expense reimbursement programs, company cars, up to $185 per month of free parking, etc.

But pass-through entities, too, can provide benefits such as retirement plans and health plans. Although owners don't get tax-free treatment for health coverage, they can deduct the premiums from gross income on their individual returns (70% in 2002 and 100% in 2003).

Consult an expert to make sure you're making full use of tax-favored fringe benefits available given your situation.

• ***Make discount valuation gifts.*** To reduce potential future estate taxes—make *discount valuation gifts* of interests in the business or in business assets to those family members.

The annual gift tax exclusion allows tax-free gifts of up to $11,000 per recipient in 2002 and 2003—$22,000 when gifts are made by a married couple.

But when a gift is made of a minority interest in a private business, valuation discounts may be taken to reduce the amount of the gift. These discounts may reach 30% or 40% for lack of marketability and the lack of control conveyed by a minority interest.

EXAMPLE: Real estate worth $300,000 is owned by a limited partnership (LP). More than 10% ownership of the LP can be transferred by a single gift of $21,000 using a 30% minority discount.

The minority discount applies to each gift of a minority interest, even if several separate gifts together transfer majority ownership of a business.

The original owner of a business can retain control over it even after transferring majority ownership to others—for instance continuing to act as general partner of an LP or manager of an LLC after the transfer.

Consult with your tax adviser for details.

■

A BOOKISH IDEA

Source: **Malcolm Katt,** an antiques dealer and owner of Millwood Gallery in Millwood, New York.

Sell used books on-line through Amazon.com. At *www.amazon.com* go to "Sell Your Stuff." Enter the ISBN number of the book—found near the bar code. Select a condition—such as "like new" or "very good"—and set a price. You can use Amazon's suggested price or name your own. When the book sells, Amazon informs you and processes payment—less a 15% commission and 99 cents. You pack and ship the book yourself.

■

RETIREMENT

REBUILDING YOUR RETIREMENT DREAM

Source: **Laurence I. Foster, CPA/PFS,** former partner and currently consultant at Eisner LLP, 750 Third Ave., New York City 10017. He is chairman of The Personal Financial Specialist Credential Committee at the American Institute of Certified Public Accountants.

A bear market can slash the value of investors' portfolios and threaten many retirement plans. If you're close to retirement—or already retired—when this happens, recast your plans to overcome the market slump…

• ***Rethink your retirement age.*** I have clients whose plans to retire young never were realistic. Now I tell them, "You no longer have the money to think about retiring at 60. Plan to retire at 65 instead." **STRATEGIES…**

• Expect to keep working until you can *afford* to retire, even if you must forgo early retirement.

• Stay where you work now for as long as you need to. Unless there's company-wide downsizing, you generally can't be forced out because of age. Or...find a similar job with a different employer.

EXAMPLE: A client of mine was a special agent with the Internal Revenue Service. He retired in his 40s and took a similar job with New York State. He plans to work long enough at the new job to give him a second pension.

• ***Work part-time to flesh out your retirement savings.*** Instead of a full-time job that's a long commute from home, work four days a week in the neighborhood.

EXAMPLE: I know a sales manager for a large company who had to retire early. He loved working with his hands, so he started a handyman business. The income from that, plus his pension, supports him very nicely.

• ***Contribute more to your retirement plans.*** You can now contribute more to retirement savings plans. I tell clients, "Spend less, save more and make the new maximum contributions to all your plans." **HERE ARE THE NEW CAPS...**

401(K) PLANS: Maximum annual contribution in 2002 is $11,000 and goes up to $15,000 in 2006.

IRAS: Maximum annual contribution goes up from $3,000 in 2002 to $5,000 in 2008.

CATCH-UP CONTRIBUTIONS: Anyone age 50 or older can now make annual catch-up contributions to a retirement plan. The maximum extra contribution is $1,000 to a 401(k) plan and $500 to an IRA. Maximum catch-up contributions will increase in future years.

• ***Stretch your budget by spending less.*** Spending patterns become so ingrained that expenses that easily could be eliminated are treated as obligatory. **PAINLESS WAYS TO CUT BACK...**

• Automobiles. Instead of leasing a car and turning it over every two years, it's more economical to buy a car and keep it for five or six years.

• Dining out. Empty nesters eat out more often—sometimes every night. Limit dining out to twice a week. Eat earlier to catch the early bird special.

• Life insurance. You bought life insurance when you had a family to care for. But the children are on their own now and your retirement savings will provide for your spouse. If you cash in the policy, you'll eliminate a big annual expense. If there is a large surrender value, you gain a one-time addition to retirement savings. Discuss other alternatives with your financial adviser.

CAUTION: This may generate tax if you get back more than you paid for the policy.

• ***Rethink your plans for children and grandchildren.*** When times were good, you might have made plans to pay for college for your grandkids. Times aren't good anymore, so maybe those plans must change. After all, the grandkids can always get loans for college, but no one will lend you money to live on in retirement.

CHALLENGE: It's not easy to back out of promises made to children and grandchildren. Rely on your family to understand that you made those promises of assistance in good faith under different economic conditions.

• ***Rethink your investment strategy.*** Bear markets usually do not last forever. Historically, stocks rally, and you could well recover most—maybe all—of your losses.

A mistake now might be to dump stocks and seek safety in cash. You could miss the market turnaround and lose out on substantial gains. A good allocation for someone a few years from retirement may still be 70% to 80% stocks and 20% to 30% bonds or cash, depending on your risk tolerance.

SAFEST STRATEGY: If you have investments with strong long-term prospects, dollar-cost-average your way into more shares at today's depressed prices. If there's nothing you want to buy today, build up cash to invest once the market clearly has turned around.

Either way, the next market recovery should greatly increase the value of those investments you bought at today's low prices.

RISKIER STRATEGY: If you're comfortable taking risks and your work gives you insights into when an industry might turn around, consider bargain hunting among stocks in that industry.

Don't be greedy. Set a target at which to sell. If the price is $5 a share now, sell when the price hits $8 or $10. You've put some money in your pocket that will make your retirement more secure. Because you bought cheaply, your long-term risk is low. No one loses out by selling a few dollars below the "high."

• ***Use your home to bolster retirement savings.*** A married couple can take a tax-free capital gain of up to $500,000 on the sale of their home if it was their primary residence for two out of the five years prior to sale.

If you own a residence and a vacation home, sell the residence and take advantage of the $500,000 exclusion. Move into the vacation home, live there for two years, sell that home and once again use the $500,000 exclusion.

• ***Rethink your plans for withdrawing savings.*** By law, you must begin withdrawing money from most retirement plans each year after you turn 70½. To calculate your minimum distribution, check your age and how much you have in the plan against the IRS table in the supplement to IRS Publication 590 at *www.irs.gov.*

If your nest egg has shrunk, the amount you can withdraw from other retirement investments shrinks as well. If you must keep selling stocks in a weak market to generate the money to meet your expenses in retirement, your whole nest egg could vanish quickly.

WHAT TO DO: Increase your allocation to cash or money market funds as you near retirement. You can withdraw enough from these funds to live on without having to dump stocks in a weak market.

Analyze how much income you'll need in retirement. Then shift from stocks with low income to higher income investments until withdrawals will allow you to live at the minimum acceptable level. You might have to shift a substantial amount of your portfolio into fixed-income investments to guarantee you will always have the money you need to live on.

With most of your withdrawal needs taken care of from income investments, you then can take more chances with your stocks in hopes of a higher return.

■

HOW TO GUARD YOUR RETIREMENT NEST EGG

Source: **Don Phillips,** managing director of the financial research firm Morningstar, Inc., 225 W. Wacker Dr., Chicago 60606.

The collapse of Enron, which left tens of thousands of investors and former employees holding shares worth next to nothing, is dispiriting. It came on top of a tough two years in the market.

LESSON TO ALL: Diversify, especially if you're retired or nearing retirement. Diversify your portfolio. Diversify your 401(k) investments.

MISSION CRITICAL YEARS...

The years just prior to and after retirement are "mission critical" years. The most important thing for investors then is to avoid making any big mistakes.

Always keep a margin of safety in your investments. That means limiting exposure to any one stock, market sector or asset class.

In the Enron debacle, employees were prevented from selling company stock out of their 401(k) plans while corporate officers dumped hundreds of millions of dollars of their Enron holdings. Enron workers were "locked in" for several weeks while there was a change in 401(k) plan managers. Even so, many Enron employees were too heavily invested in the company's stock. Some lost their entire life savings.

Many US companies make their matching 401(k) contributions in company stock. There are often restrictions governing when employees can sell that stock. Usually, you can divest company shares after age 50 or before retirement.

Take advantage of these opportunities to lighten your exposure to company stock, even if the company is doing well and you have no reason to suspect trouble ahead.

If you have been receiving company stock as a match for your 401(k) contributions, avoid putting any personal funds into that stock.

GOAL: No more than 10% invested in your employer's (or any one) stock. After all, you don't want your job, health insurance, pension benefits and savings nest egg all subject to the fortunes of one company.

IDENTIFY INCOME NEEDS...

Instead of using a formula to calculate how much to invest in which asset classes, start with your income needs. Then worry about how your assets should be divided.

How much can you count on from Social Security? Pension benefits? How much could you add by, say, investing in municipal bonds or treasuries laddered to mature at regular dates in the future?

For those who need a flow of income to sleep soundly at night, it may pay to invest a lump sum in an annuity. While there may be high fees, at least you'll know that you won't outlive your money.

The biggest risk with annuities is that inflation may erode your buying power. That's why everyone should own some common stocks. They have the potential to increase in value and total return.

Most people roll over their 401(k) into a self-administered IRA when they retire. The percentage of your portfolio to put in stocks depends on your age, overall resources and ability to tolerate risk.

SPREAD RISK AROUND...

Take several small risks instead of one major risk. Bonds, for example, involve several types of risk—credit risk...interest rate risk (prices fall as rates rise)...and, in the case of Ginnie Maes (GNMAs), prepayment risk.

With GNMAs, when rates fall, homeowners pay off or refinance their mortgages, leaving investors to reinvest at lower rates.

STRATEGY: Choose a bond fund that is already diversified among the different types of bond risk.

The T. Rowe Price Spectrum Income Fund (RPSIX), for example, is made up of other T. Rowe Price funds, including domestic bond funds, international bond funds, a money market fund and an income-oriented stock fund. 800-225-5132.

OTHER FUND CHOICES...

For those who prefer a traditional 60% stocks and 40% bonds allocation, I recommend the following allocation for the stock portion...

- *30%*—large-cap stocks in an index fund.
- *10%*—small- and mid-cap value stocks.
- *10%*—small- and mid-cap growth stock funds.
- *10%*—international funds.

For the 40% fixed-income portfolio, my selections would be...

- *15%*—government bonds in a low-expense fund.
- *10%*—investment-grade corporate bond fund.
- *10%*—high-yield (junk) bond fund.
- *5%*—international bond fund.

For investors who feel more comfortable with a 40% stock and 60% bond allocation, reduce my stock fund choices appropriately and add more bond funds. Do *not* put more than 5% in international bonds.

■

SOUND REASONS TO CONSIDER WITHDRAWING FROM YOUR IRA BEFORE THE LAW SAYS YOU MUST

Source: **Ed Slott, CPA,** E. Slott & Co., CPAs, 100 Merrick Rd., Suite 200 E, Rockville Centre, New York 11570. *www.irahelp.com.*

It's usually a good idea to leave retirement funds in an IRA for as long as possible.

REASON: To maximize the benefit of tax-deferred compound investment returns.

But this is not always the best strategy—especially if your IRA holds more funds than you will need for your own support and you hope to leave IRA funds to your heirs. **PROBLEMS...**

- ***IRA distributions are taxed at top ordinary rates*** of up to 38.6% in 2002 and 2003—even if paid from capital gains that would be taxed at no more than 20% if realized outside the IRA.

TRAP: As you grow older, your required minimum annual distribution increases each year—so you may be compelled to withdraw funds and pay this tax even if you don't need IRA income.

• ***If you die owning a valuable IRA, it may be subject to double taxation.*** First, the IRA itself may be subject to estate tax at rates up to 50% (declining over the next several years). Then distributions from the IRA to heirs will be subject to income tax at up to 38.6% in 2002 and 2003—plus state and local taxes. Combined tax rates may exceed 85%!

ALTERNATIVE: Consider taking funds out of an IRA early and reinvesting them in normal investment accounts. **BENEFITS...**

• Future gains you realize to support your own needs may be subject to tax at lower capital gains rates.

• Investments you hold until you die may escape both estate and income tax. **THAT'S BECAUSE...**

...investments held until death (at least for the next eight years) receive "stepped-up basis," eliminating all accumulated taxable capital gain on them.

...you'll obtain much more flexibility to make tax-free gifts of the funds to heirs, and to take other estate planning steps, to reduce your estate to below a taxable size.

ALSO: You may be able to invest the former IRA funds in other assets that better meet family needs than an IRA—such as life insurance, the proceeds of which are income tax free and may escape estate tax if the policy is held by a properly structured life insurance trust.

PLANNING: Consider your likely future income and estate tax liabilities now. See if paying a tax bill on IRA withdrawals now may save paying much more in taxes later.

If so, consider withdrawal options starting at age 59½, when early distribution penalties no longer apply.

Also avoid overcontributing to an IRA.

EXAMPLE: When you leave a company owning its stock in the qualified retirement plan, consider taking a direct distribution of the stock from the plan rather than rolling it over into an IRA. The taxable income on the distribution will equal only the value of the stock when it was contributed to your retirement account—and you will retain tax-favored capital gains treatment for all its appreciation in value.

IMPORTANT: Every situation is different. Consult an expert. ■

FOR A WORRY-FREE RETIREMENT BUY SAVINGS BONDS

Source: **Richard J. Shapiro, Esq.**, tax partner, Ernst & Young LLP, 787 Seventh Ave., New York City 10019.

Don't overlook US savings bonds when building a nest egg for your retirement. They're not a bad investment today. You can't lose principal, as you easily can in the stock market, and the interest rate is competitive with other safe investments. Plus...savings bonds have built-in tax advantages.

Positive features of savings bonds...

- ***They're easy to buy.***
- ***You pay no commission or fees.***
- ***They're perfectly safe.***
- ***Interest rates compare favorably*** with the rates on five-year CDs and Treasury bonds.
- ***You can defer paying tax on the interest*** until you redeem the bonds.
- ***They work well with any estate plan.***

VARIETIES...

There are two kinds of US savings bonds...

- ***I bonds*** are sold at face value in denominations ranging from $50 to $10,000. These pay two types of interest—a fixed rate that remains constant throughout the life of the bond and a rate that is adjusted every six months (on May 1 and November 1) depending on the rate of inflation.
- ***EE bonds*** are sold at a discount of half their face value in the same denominations as I bonds—a $50 EE bond costs $25. EE bonds issued on or after May 1, 1997, earn 90% of the five-year Treasury bond rate for the prior six months.

The new *Patriot bonds,* issued after December 11, 2001, are simply EE bonds bearing a special legend. In all other respects, Patriot bonds are the same as EE bonds.

YIELDS, REDEMPTIONS, LIMITS...

COMPETITIVE YIELDS: I bonds currently yield 4.08%. EE bonds yield 3.25%. This compares with an average rate of 3.76% on five-year CDs. Average yields on Treasury bonds are now 3.25% on the five-year and 4.375% on the 10-year.

REDEMPTIONS: While savings bonds earn interest for 30 years, they can be cashed in as early as six months after purchase. But there's a three-month interest penalty for redemptions within five years of purchase. Because of this, savings bonds are best used for long-term investments.

ANNUAL PURCHASE LIMITS: Federal law limits the amount you can invest each year in savings bonds to $30,000 (I bonds) and $15,000 (EE bonds). However, gifts you make of savings bonds are not counted toward these dollar limits (even though your Social Security number appears on the gift bond). The I and EE bond limits are separate—you can invest both $30,000 in I bonds and $15,000 in EE bonds in the same year.

You can buy savings bonds through local banks, payroll savings plans or on-line at *www.savingsbonds.gov,* where you can charge purchases of up to $5,000 to a credit card—Discover, MasterCard or Visa.

DEFERRED, EXEMPT AND FREE...

Savings bonds offer unique tax incentives that enhance their investment value...

• ***Income tax deferral.*** You don't have to report savings bond interest annually, though you can if you want to. This would make sense if your income was so low that no tax was due. Interest can be deferred for as long as you hold the bond, up to the final maturity date.

• ***Exemption from state and local income taxes.*** Interest on US savings bonds is never subject to state or local income taxes. That's an advantage for investors in states with income tax.

• ***Free of federal tax if used for college tuition.*** Savings bond interest is tax free if the bonds are redeemed to pay tuition and other qualified higher education costs for the bondholder or his/her spouse or dependent, as long as the bondholder's income is below a set amount.

To the extent that savings bonds are used for college expenses, other resources need not be touched and can build up for retirement savings.

USING SAVINGS BONDS IN RETIREMENT...

• ***Cashing out.*** I bonds and EE bonds only accrue interest—they do not pay out interest currently. They must be cashed in to obtain retirement income. If you've purchased bonds throughout your working years, they won't come due all at once and can be held until their final maturity date. If you purchase bonds in your 40s, for example, they'll be available for retirement income in your 70s.

• ***Early redemption strategy.*** If you want to cash them in prior to maturity, time redemptions to maximize interest. For bonds issued before May 1, 1997, cash in bonds just after their semiannual interest date so you don't lose out on six months of interest.

EXAMPLE: You bought an EE bond on January 15, 1995. If you want to redeem it, do so after May 1 or November 1—the dates on which interest for the prior six months is credited. If you cash it in on April 30, you lose interest back to November 1 of the prior year (you receive interest credited only through October 31).

For bonds issued after April 30, 1997, cash in bonds as early in the month as possible. Interest accrues on the first day of the month—regardless of which day in the month you originally purchased the bond.

• ***Changing the way you report interest.*** If your tax rate drops in retirement, you can switch from deferring interest to reporting it annually. You must report all of the accrued interest to date, though. The following year, you must report only the interest accrual in that year.

EASY ESTATE PLANNING...

While your primary purpose in owning savings bonds may be retirement income, you can work them into your estate plan if you don't need the funds for retirement.

• ***Naming a beneficiary.*** When you purchase a bond, you can designate a beneficiary who will inherit the bond upon your death. Since the bond passes directly to the beneficiary, it is not subject to probate expenses.

CAUTION: Adding or deleting another person's name as co-owner does not result in immediate taxation. Similarly, transferring a bond into a living trust does not cause accrued interest to be immediately taxable.

But gifting a bond to someone else who changes the registration of the bond from your name to his is considered a redemption—all accrued interest becomes immediately taxable. This same result occurs if you transfer a bond into a trust in which you give up all rights of ownership.

• ***Executor's option on accrued interest.*** If you've been deferring interest, the accrued amount can be taxed on your final income tax return or continue to be deferred. It's up to your executor.

Your executor would want to report the accrued interest on your last return if it resulted in little or no additional income tax. This would likely be the case if you died early in the year (and so had little other income to report that year)...or if there were losses to report on the final return (the losses will offset the bond interest).

If your executor makes this election, your beneficiaries will be taxed only on interest accruing after your death.

If your executor does not make the election, your beneficiary can opt to report the interest annually—including all accrued interest to date—or continue deferral until the bond matures or is redeemed.

■

TAXES

THE GENERAL RULE MAY NOT BE BEST FOR YOU

Source: **Lisa N. Collins, CPA/PFS,** vice president and director of tax services, Harding, Shymanski & Co., PC, Evansville, Indiana, and author of *The Complete Idiot's Guide to Tax Deductions.* Alpha. She is a member of the steering committee of the American Institute of Certified Public Accountants' Tax Strategies for the High Income Individual Conference.

Tax experts are quick to quote the "general rule" that applies in various situations. But sometimes it's better to ignore these general rules—and do the opposite. **EXAMPLES...**

STRATEGIES FOR INDIVIDUALS...

• ***Income deferral.*** It is a generally accepted practice to defer as much income as possible into subsequent tax years. By doing so, you'll postpone current tax on that income.

Deferral makes a lot of sense now, when tax rates are falling. Not only will tax be postponed, but the deferred income will be taxed at lower rates.

However, in some situations, accelerating income into the *current* year is the better strategy.

Taxpayers should accelerate income when they...

• Are subject to the alternative minimum tax (AMT) and are in a tax bracket above 28% for regular income tax. Income for AMT purposes is taxed at only 28%. Any income you accelerate will be taxed at this rate rather than your higher regular income tax rate.

• Have deductions, credits or carryovers that could be claimed only if income were accelerated. These write-offs will offset the accelerated income (or the tax on that income).

• ***Deferred compensation.*** Executives are usually advised to arrange with their employer to defer year-end bonuses and other compensation into their retirement years, if possible, when they should be in a lower tax bracket.

But deferral does *not* make sense if...

• There is any concern about the company's survival. *Problem with deferred compensation:* For the deferral to be effective for tax purposes, the arrangement must be an unsecured promise by the company to make payment. The funds remain subject to the claims of the company's general creditors if the company runs into trouble. *Impact:* Your deferred compensation could be lost in bankruptcy.

• You believe you can earn more on the money by investing it yourself than the company will pay. For example, the company may credit an annual amount of interest on the deferred compensation, but if you can earn more than this rate, it's better to take the money, pay the tax now and invest for the future.

• ***IRA distributions.*** The general advice is to take only minimum distributions from traditional IRAs. That way, the funds can continue to grow on a tax-deferred basis. You're told not to take money until age 70½ (the required beginning date for distributions), and then only enough to avoid penalty.

But it's better to take more than the required amounts if...

• You intend to make substantial charitable donations. Bigger IRA distributions will increase your adjusted gross income (AGI), allowing a greater current deduction for the donations. The deduction will help offset the income resulting from the IRA distribution.

• You are in a low tax bracket. For example, a person who retires at age 60 may have most of his/her money tied up in a rollover IRA account and little or no other income. Such a person probably should take distributions right away—even though not legally required—because this income will be taxed at low rates.

NOTE: After age 59½, IRA withdrawals are no longer subject to an early distribution penalty.

• ***Dependency exemption.*** Parents can claim a dependency exemption for a child under age 19 (or under age 24 and a full-time student), regardless of the child's income.

In the case of divorced parents, the dependency exemption automatically belongs to the custodial parent. But the custodial parent can waive the exemption in favor of the noncustodial parent—who is often the parent providing the greater share of support. Divorce decrees often require such a waiver, and this is the general rule.

*But...*the custodial parent should not waive the exemption if the noncustodial parent is a high-income taxpayer subject to the phase-out of the exemption. In 2002, the exemption is phased out when AGI exceeds $137,300 for a single parent who is not a head of household ($139,500 in 2003).

Starting in 2006, the phase-out of personal exemptions for high-income taxpayers starts to disappear and is eliminated entirely by 2010.

• ***State and local taxes.*** The general rule is that you should pay before the end of the year any state and local taxes otherwise due the following January.

REASON: To increase write-offs for the current year.

*But...*you should *not* prepay state and local taxes if you are subject to the alternative minimum tax. These taxes are *not* deductible for AMT purposes.

STRATEGIES FOR BUSINESS...

• ***Depreciation.*** The general advice is to claim accelerated depreciation to boost business write-offs. But doing so can dilute the benefit of the write-offs and, in some cases, trigger AMT.

• Start-up businesses should "save" depreciation deductions for future years by opting for slower current depreciation.

• Don't elect first-year expensing (Section 179 deduction) in a year when the business has an operating loss. The deduction can only be claimed when there is an equal amount of taxable income (although unused expensing can be carried forward). Instead, claim depreciation to spread the write-offs into profitable years.

• ***Net operating losses (NOLs).*** The general rule requires NOLs to be carried back (generally two years, but five years in 2002) and then forward for up to 20 years. A carryback produces an immediate cash infusion for the business. But taxpayers can elect not to claim the carryback and instead only carry NOLs forward. **THIS ELECTION SHOULD BE CONSIDERED WHEN...**

• You expect to be in a higher tax bracket in the future. This will allow the NOLs to effectively save more tax dollars.

• You were married in a carryback year. *Example:* A taxpayer generating an NOL was married in a carryback year but is single in the loss year. Waiving the carryback avoids complicated computations and possible dealings with his former spouse.

STRATEGIES FOR INVESTORS...

• ***Capital gains and losses.*** The standard advice is to postpone realization of capital gains until assets have been held for more than one year. This makes the gains long-term capital gains, which are taxed at favorable rates. But waiting isn't always necessary.

If you have capital losses—long term or short term—you don't have to wait out the year to realize long-term gains. You can use short-term gains—as well as long-term gains—to offset your capital losses.

• ***Savings bonds.*** Taxpayers owning US savings bonds generally opt to postpone reporting income until the bonds are cashed in, or mature. But reporting interest currently may be wise when the bondholder...

• Dies early in the year. The accrued interest on the bonds may be taxed at low rates if the decedent had little or no other income in the year he died. *Reason:* In the year of death, a decedent can claim a full standard deduction (if not itemizing deductions) and a full personal exemption—no proration required.

• Is a child over age 13. Once a child is beyond the kiddie tax, income is taxed at his low rates—10% or 15%. A child with modest income may pay no tax on the interest.

CAUTION: If the child has been deferring interest until age 13 and his adviser now wants him to report it currently, the child must file for a change in accounting method. Automatic IRS consent procedures simplify this action.

• ***Installment sales.*** The general rule is to use the installment method to report gain on sales of assets for which payment will be received in more than one year. **BUT ELECTING OUT OF INSTALLMENT REPORTING IS ADVISABLE WHEN...**

• You have capital losses to offset the gain. Don't overlook carryover capital losses that you can use to offset the gain.

• The seller dies in the year of the sale, before payments have been received. Electing out of the installment sale method causes the entire gain to be taxed on the final tax return of the decedent. The income tax obligation reduces the estate tax (because it is a liability of the decedent).

If the gain is not reported on the final tax return, the heirs will have to pay income tax on the installment gain (because it is income in respect of a decedent). This is in addition to paying estate tax on the value of the installment note.

■

PROVEN WAY TO AVOID IRS PENALTIES

Source: Kevin P. Osborne, TC Memo 2002-11.

If you use a professional to prepare your tax return, not only will it be less likely to contain errors that could result in penalties, you may also escape penalties for errors that it *does* contain.

EXAMPLE: When a business proprietor claimed several deductions that proved to be erroneous, the IRS sought to impose negligence penalties as well as back taxes.

TAX COURT: The individual had provided all his records to a reputable tax professional and had relied on the professional's advice when preparing his return. So he had acted responsibly, and the penalty was lifted.

■

TAX FORM LOOPHOLES

Source: **Edward Mendlowitz, CPA,** partner, Mendlowitz Weitsen, LLP, CPAs, Two Pennsylvania Plaza, Suite 1500, New York City 10121.

Most people simply try to get the numbers right when they fill out their returns. But there's a lot more to it. Making strategic decisions can save you money and, if you're careful, can reduce the odds of an IRS audit. **CONSIDER THESE STRATEGIES...**

FOR INDIVIDUAL TAXPAYERS...

LOOPHOLE: Make a Section 83(b) election when you exercise unvested incentive stock options. The election has to be made within 30 days of the exercise and will lower your alternative minimum tax (AMT) liability.

Making a Section 83(b) election means you owe AMT—in the year you make the election—on the difference between the exercise price for the options and the fair market value of the shares.

If you don't make the election, the AMT is calculated on the difference between the price you pay for the options and the fair market value of the shares when they vest.

STRATEGY: If you expect the shares to increase substantially in value, exercise incentive stock options as soon as possible. That way, you minimize the difference between the exercise price and the shares' market value.

LOOPHOLE: File a gift tax return for gifts used to pay insurance premiums. File the return even though it is not legally required.

When you give money to a trust to pay insurance premiums, no gift tax return is required if you give less than $11,000 in 2002 and 2003 and no grandchildren are involved (as long as the recipient signs the "Crummey" letter, making the payment a gift of a present interest).

If the IRS determines in a subsequent estate tax audit that the letter was inadequate, no statute of limitations will have run. The donor or his/her estate could be liable for tax on the gifts.

BETTER: Filing a gift tax return blocks the IRS from assessing taxes after the three-year statute of limitations runs.

LOOPHOLE: Don't take valuation discounts on Form 709 for small gifts. When you take a valuation discount for a gift, you must check the box on the gift tax return and include full disclosure of the reasons for the discount.

If you don't take a discount, the box is not checked and you will decrease the chances of an audit. You should compare the benefits of avoiding an audit with the higher gift valuation.

LOOPHOLE: Enter Form 1099 information on Schedules B and D of your tax return—even if it's wrong. The IRS cross-checks the totals shown on Schedules B and D, reflecting capital gains, dividends and interest income, with the amounts banks, brokers and other payors report on Forms 1099. If the amounts differ, an IRS notice is automatically generated.

IF THERE'S A MISTAKE ON A 1099: Enter the 1099 figure on your tax return. Then subtract the erroneous amount to end up with your real total. Attach an explanatory letter to your return.

LOOPHOLE: Claim no more than nine withholding exemptions on Form W-4.

When you claim 10 or more withholding allowances, or exemptions from withholding, a copy of the Form W-4 must be sent to the IRS, where agents can check whether the exemptions are valid and possibly generate correspondence.

LOOPHOLE: Make a tardy generation-skipping transfer election. In general, grandparents who set up trusts for grandchildren in 2002 can take a $1.1 million lifetime exemption, adjusted for inflation, for their collective gifts. When Form 709 is filed on time, the value of the gift is determined when the gift (or transfer) was actually made. When you make a late election, the value is determined when you filed the late return and elected to offset the gift's value against the lifetime exemption.

So, making a post–April 15 election saves money when the value of the gift decreases after you make it, such as a whole-life insurance policy premium.

TRAP: If you don't make a timely election and the insured dies, the full face value of the policy's face could be considered a generation-skipping transfer. That could create an enormous tax bill.

LOOPHOLE: Keep the total of your money held in foreign bank accounts below $10,000. You must file Form TD F 90-22.1 when the aggregate of foreign bank accounts in which you hold money and accounts from which you have check-signing power (even though the money is not yours) exceeds $10,000. Filing the form opens the accounts up for IRS scrutiny.

FOR BUSINESS TAXPAYERS...

LOOPHOLE: Choose a low-audit business code number to put on the company's Schedule C. The IRS targets for audit certain types of businesses and industries. When your business could legitimately fit into more than one category, choose the business code number that is not on the IRS's hit list. For example, a car wash can possibly be called an auto service center.

LOOPHOLE: Attach an "election schedule" for a controlled group of corporations to the corporation's Form 1120. When you run a controlled group of corporations (more than one corporation under common ownership), you must attach to the business's tax return an election schedule that includes an apportionment plan for certain tax items (e.g., the AMT exemption). Otherwise, the IRS automatically allocates all exemptions and the benefits of the lower tax brackets equally among all the companies in the group.

STRATEGY: When you have a controlled group that includes dormant and active businesses, allocate all the exemptions and tax breaks to the active business.

LOOPHOLE: Report a fair market value appraisal on Form 1120S when you switch your C corporation to an S corporation. This will reduce the taxes owed on any built-in gains.

Businesses that convert from C corp to S corp status are required to value the business's assets as of the date of the conversion. If assets are sold within 10 years, profits are realized as if the C status were still in effect to the extent of any built-in gains as of that date, i.e., the S corporation pays the tax.

STRATEGY: When you get a preconversion *fair market value* appraisal, the valuation is generally lower than what the assets could be sold for, saving taxes if the assets are sold before the 10-year deadline.

■

CAN'T PAY YOUR TAXES? IRS INSTALLMENT AGREEMENTS AND OFFERS IN COMPROMISE CAN BE VERY HELPFUL

Source: **Stephen R. Buschel, CPA,** tax partner, BDO Seidman, LLP, 300 Madison Ave., New York City 10017.

Can't afford to pay the taxes you owe to the IRS when they are due? You may be able to get more time to pay through an *installment agreement.*

If you won't *ever* be able to pay the taxes you owe—because you simply don't have the money or because paying would result in serious hardship—you may be able to negotiate a reduction of the outstanding balance through an *offer in compromise* (OIC).

The IRS has liberalized the use of both installment agreements and OICs. More taxpayers are using them than ever before—although they still aren't the best option for everybody.

Here's what you need to know about installment agreements and OICs—and how to tell whether one is right for you.

GETTING MORE TIME...

An installment agreement simply gives you additional time to pay the tax you owe—plus interest and penalties.

The liberalized rules for installment agreements allow you to obtain one automatically if the tax involved does not exceed $10,000 *and* you are current on all previous tax obligations.

Apply for an agreement by filing IRS Form 9465, *Installment Agreement Request.* You can file it with your tax return if you can't afford the balance due on it, or in response to a bill for past-due taxes sent by the IRS.

There is a fee of $43 for using Form 9465, which the IRS wraps into the agreement—don't pay it separately.

If the unpaid tax exceeds $10,000, approval by the IRS is *not* automatic. The IRS will want to know that you are paying all you can, and you may have to negotiate the agreement's terms. In doing so, the IRS will look at your past record of tax compliance as well as at your assets.

USEFUL: The IRS's Interactive Installment Payment Process can show you the terms of an agreement for which you will qualify. Request an automatically approved agreement. It will estimate the monthly payment and number of months in the term. If the tax involves more than $10,000, you can learn terms the IRS may find acceptable.

In the search box for the IRS Web site, *www.irs.gov,* enter "Interactive Installment Payment Process."

If tax exceeds $10,000 and you prepare a Form 9465 application (or subsequently negotiate terms with the IRS), get help from a tax professional who is experienced in arranging installment agreements. He/she should understand the technicalities involved and know how to get the best terms for you.

STRATEGY: With an installment agreement, you will end up paying the entire tax you owe *plus* interest and penalties. This means you could pay more in total than you would if you borrowed from a bank or other lender to pay the tax bill.

BOTTOM LINE: It's usually best to borrow from another lender to pay the IRS. Use an IRS installment agreement as a last option.

REDUCING A TAX BILL...

If you can't pay a tax bill—and never will be able to pay—your best move may be to make an offer in compromise to the IRS.

If the IRS accepts your OIC, a partial payment of the tax you owe will result in full settlement of your bill, giving you a fresh start.

The IRS has reduced the technical requirements for processing OICs and now is granting them on expanded grounds, including hardship.

Getting an OIC still is not an easy task. Because the IRS is waiving taxes, interest and penalties when it accepts an OIC, the application process is more extensive than with an installment agreement—and the IRS will examine your finances more thoroughly.

The IRS will accept an OIC only if it finds one or more of the following...

- ***Doubt as to collectibility of the tax you owe***—meaning the IRS is convinced that you will never be able to pay the tax.

• ***Doubt as to liability for the tax***—the IRS thinks there is a chance you could escape paying the tax through litigation.

• ***Issues of "effective tax administration"***—collecting the tax will cause you undue hardship, or will be fundamentally unfair in some way.

EXAMPLE: A retiree has sufficient funds in his IRA to pay his tax bill, but doing so would deplete the IRA and leave him with no retirement income. The IRS may consider this a hardship justification for accepting an OIC.

REQUESTING AN OIC...

File IRS Form 656, *Offer in Compromise*. You must also file an extensive financial disclosure statement—IRS Form 433-A for individuals or Form 433-B for businesses.

After you submit these forms, the IRS will review your situation to make sure the information on the forms is correct... and to get a better picture of your financial circumstances.

The amount by which the IRS may be willing to compromise the total amount you owe will depend on...

• ***Your total assets.***

• ***Your income now and your future income-earning capability.***

• ***Your essential living expenses.***

The IRS also will consider whether an OIC will enable it to collect funds that it wouldn't be able to reach otherwise.

EXAMPLE: You offer to borrow funds from a rich uncle to make a compromise payment of your taxes now. The uncle isn't liable for your taxes, so the IRS can't get that money any other way. If it believes it may be better off by taking this money in the compromise now, rather than by sending your entire tax bill through a lengthy collection process with uncertain results, it may accept the OIC.

The IRS has established standards to determine what it deems appropriate essential living costs. These cover food, housing, clothing, transportation costs, etc., for families of different sizes.

The IRS uses these standards to evaluate a taxpayer's ability to pay a delinquent tax bill. It generally considers income in excess of the standard amounts to be available to pay tax. These Collection Financial Standards are available on the IRS

Web site under its On-line Offer in Compromise Program. On the IRS home page, *www.irs.gov,* click on "Individuals."

APPEALS: If the IRS refuses your OIC, it will explain why in writing. If your offer was too low, the IRS will indicate an amount that it would find acceptable.

You can appeal such a rejection to the IRS Appeals Division. Or you can make a new OIC based on information learned from the IRS's rejection of the previous OIC.

IMPORTANT: An OIC may be the most important tax transaction of your life. Draft it with the help of a tax professional who is experienced in using the collection standards and in handling subsequent negotiations with the IRS.

■

MILLIONS OVERPAY TAXES BY FAILING TO ITEMIZE

Source: General Accounting Office report GAO-02-509, *Further Estimates of Taxpayers Who May Have Overpaid Federal Taxes by Not Itemizing, www.gao.gov.*

Each year, only about 30% of taxpayers itemize deductions—but more should.

A new study finds that as many as 2.2 million filers could have cut their tax bills by claiming itemized deductions (for items such as mortgage interest, property taxes, state and local taxes, and charitable contributions). But they, or their preparers, failed to do so and used the simpler standard deduction instead. Their overpayments may have totaled almost $1 billion.

If you didn't itemize a return within the last three years, check to see if the total itemized deductions you could have claimed exceeded the standard deduction. If so, file IRS Form 1040X, *Amended US Individual Income Tax Return,* to take your extra deductions now—and get a tax refund.

■

EDUCATION EXPENSE LOOPHOLES

Source: **Edward Mendlowitz, CPA,** partner, Mendlowitz Weitsen, LLP, CPAs, Two Pennsylvania Plaza, Suite 1500, New York City 10121.

To ease the burden of college costs, incentives were enacted in the *Tax Relief Act of 2001.* Here are the main changes, along with other tax-wise ways to cut your education costs...

LOOPHOLE: Accumulate tax-free tuition money. You can do this with a Section 529 savings plan or "qualified state tuition program" (QSTP)—they're one and the same. These state-sponsored investment programs give families tax breaks as they save for college expenses.

Money withdrawn from 529 accounts to pay tuition and related expenses is now *tax free.*

HOW THEY WORK: Contributions to the plans are considered gifts, and qualify for the $11,000 annual gift tax exclusion that's in effect for 2002. You can elect to treat a $55,000 contribution to a single beneficiary in one year ($110,000 when spouses "split" gifts) as having been made in equal payments over five years. That way, the entire contribution is gift tax free, even though it exceeds the $11,000 annual limit.

OTHER BENEFITS OF 529 PLANS: When you give money to the plan, you remove income *and* future appreciation from your taxable estate. You can set up these plans for any number of children, grandchildren or other beneficiaries whether family members or not. Go to your state's Web site to learn how to set up a 529 plan, or visit *www.collegesavings.com.*

LOOPHOLE: Take a tax deduction for education expenses. Taxpayers with incomes under $130,000 (joint) or $65,000 (single) can now claim a $3,000 above-the-line deduction for the costs of higher education. The deduction is scheduled to rise to $4,000 in 2004.

LOOPHOLE: Minimize your adjusted gross income (AGI) to avoid phaseouts of certain education tax benefits. You can do this, for one year at least, by accelerating expenses into the current year and deferring income into the next year...

- ***Qualified education loans.*** Interest of up to $2,500 on qualified education loans is fully deductible until AGI reaches $100,000 on joint tax returns. (A qualified loan is one where the proceeds are used only for qualified higher education expenses.) The interest deduction begins phasing out and then disappears when AGI exceeds $130,000. The phaseout starts at $50,000 on individual returns, and the deduction disappears when AGI exceeds $65,000.

• ***Education credits.*** The $1,500 Hope credit and the $1,000 Lifetime Learning credit phase out between AGI of $82,000 and $102,000 for joint returns ($41,000 to $51,000 for individuals) in 2002.

LOOPHOLE: Offset child-care expenses with child-care credits. Generally, couples do not qualify for child- and dependent-care credits if only one spouse works.

EXCEPTION: If one spouse is a full-time student and the other works, the couple may qualify. The law assumes that the nonworking spouse had income ($200 a month if there is one child, $400 a month if there are two or more children) and calculates the credit accordingly.

For married taxpayers, expenses that qualify for the child-care credits are limited to the lower-earning spouse's income. That would normally be the income of the parent in school, with income calculated according to the figures above. The credit is a percentage of the income.

LOOPHOLE: Take full advantage of employer educational assistance plans. When companies offer such plans, the first $5,250 of educational costs paid by your employer is tax free. Tuition, fees, books and supplies are all eligible expenses. The plan must be in writing and must be equally available to all employees.

Courses need not be job related to qualify for this tax break, so you could use the plan to help pay for a college or even a graduate degree.

LOOPHOLE: Don't pay tax on employer-reimbursed education expenses. When your employer reimburses you for education costs, you do not have to include the reimbursement on your tax return—as long as you account to your employer for the expenses. That is, you must submit bills and receipts.

LOOPHOLE: Deduct job-related education expenses. Anyone can deduct job-related education expenses for courses taken to maintain or improve the skills required in his/her present line of work. Courses that train you for a new trade or business are not deductible.

Deductible items include tuition, books, supplies and the cost of getting from your job to school. When you qualify, education expenses are treated as "miscellaneous itemized" expenses. They are deducted to the extent they exceed 2% of your AGI.

LOOPHOLE: Buy off-campus housing for your child. One way to cut your cash outlays for college living expenses is to buy a house or an apartment near the campus for your child to live in. The tax deductions the property generates will subsidize the expense.

If the property is your second residence, mortgage interest is fully deductible, as are real estate taxes.

If you rent out part of the home, it will qualify as a rental property. Your tax deductions, including depreciation, may exceed your rental income from the property, producing a loss. Up to $25,000 of these rental losses are deductible each year against your salary and other income, as long as your AGI doesn't exceed $150,000.

■

COLLEGE SAVINGS TRAP

Source: **Barbara Weltman, Esq.**, author of many books, including *Bottom Line's Very Shrewd Money Book.* Bottom Line Books. She is editor/publisher of *Barbara Weltman's Big Ideas for Small Business,* a monthly newsletter. *www.bwideas.com.*

Don't put college savings in a child's name. The standard college financial aid formula requires children to use 35% of their own assets to pay for college costs before receiving any aid. Parents are expected to contribute only up to 5.6% of their assets. Grandparents aren't required to contribute anything.

TRAP: Placing funds in a child's name to help pay for college may result in the child losing financial aid and the family paying more for the child's tuition.

BETTER: Keep college savings in your own name, then pay some college costs after the child receives tuition assistance.

■